THE PARABLE OF THE PRODIGAL SON

DISCOVER THE REAL MEANING BEHIND THE STORY!

STEPHEN J. SPYKERMAN

THE PARABLE OF THE PRODIGAL SON

© 2018 by Stephen J. Spykerman

Mount Ephraim Watchman
www.mountephraimwatchman.org

Published by Mount Ephraim Publishing

All rights reserved. No part of this book may be reproduced in any form or by any means without permission in writing from the author.

Printed in the United States of America

1st Edition -- May 2018

Edited and Arranged by Eddie R. Rogers

Front Cover Picture: Rembrandt van Rijn, *The Return of the Prodigal Son*, c. 1661–1669. 262 cm × 205 cm. Hermitage Museum, Saint Petersburg, Russia

ISBN-13: 978-1719251976
ISBN-10: 1719251975

All Bible references quoted in this booklet are taken from the New King James version, unless stated otherwise. Comments and Emphases are the author's. Readers may find that the text frequently refers to Jesus by his proper Hebrew birth name of "Yeshua," which means Salvation.

Remember the parable of the Prodigal son?

Most Christians are familiar with the parable of the *'Prodigal Son,'* which is seen as a wonderful illustration of the mercy and forgiveness of God, Our Father in Heaven. Yeshua in His parable of the *'Prodigal Son'* in Luke 15:11-32 speaks of a certain man who had two sons. His younger son asks to be given his inheritance, only to go away to a far country and waste his inherited fortune on riotous living. After living a lifestyle of self-indulgent idolatry and the pursuit of personal pleasure and abandon, he ends up totally destitute. This is the very moment a mighty famine arises in his land of exile and he is forced to take a job looking after another man's pigs! His hunger is so acute that he would have gladly filled his stomach with the husks that are fed to the swine, but no one gives him anything to eat. As he is literally perishing with hunger the prodigal son remembers how good things were when he was  still in his father's house and his heart turns toward home. Overwhelmed with remorse, he becomes convicted of his sin. Utterly humbled by his dire circumstances, he repents of his wayward lifestyle and decides to return to his father's house. His heart is filled with shame, as he recognizes that he has rejected his father and disgraced his family name. As he takes the first steps on his journey home, he decides that he is not worthy to bear his father's name any longer or to be called his son. Instead, he resolves to ask his father if he can forgive him and take him on as one of his hired workers. As he approaches his father's land, his father sees him coming from some considerable distance and runs towards him, falling on his neck and kisses him. The son then exclaims:

> "*²¹ ...Father, I have sinned against heaven and in your sight, and am no longer worthy to be called your son. ²² But the father said to his servants, Bring out the best robe and put it on him, and put a ring on his hand and sandals on his feet. ²³ And bring the fatted calf here and kill it, and let us eat and be merry; ²⁴ for this my son was dead and is alive again; he was lost and is found...*"
> (Luke 15:21-24, NKJV)

His father orders the fatted calf to be slaughtered and makes a great feast for his prodigal son. The story then goes on to relate that the faithful son, who had remained faithful and stayed at home with his father, was upset and he would not join the party. The parable goes on to relate the father's words to the older son:

> "³¹ ...***Son, you are always with me, and all that I have is yours.*** ³² ***It was right that we should make merry and be glad, for your brother was dead and is alive again, and was lost and is found.***"
> (Luke 15:31-32, NKJV)

The faithful son who stayed home with his father is upset and will not join the celebration

Christian Interpretation

The Christian interpretation of this parable is that it highlights the infinite mercy of God the Father towards the repentant sinner. The two sons being spoken of are two born again Christian believers. The younger son is attracted by the *'cares of this world'* and he is tempted to leave his father's house (the Church) to pursue a life of earthly pleasures, whilst the older son holds faithful to his calling and remains at home serving his father.

The prodigal son recklessly squanders his father's inheritance in riotous living and he ends up destitute.

The destitute prodigal son

He is forced to support himself in the meanest job possible, having to feed another man's pigs. Then a further calamity strikes as the land he is living in is afflicted by a severe famine and now his very life is in peril. Having no way out and with his

The father runs to meet his prodigal son

back against the wall, he finally recognizes the folly of his ways. With a heart full of repentance, he decides to go back to his father's house. As he sets out on his long journey hungry, unwashed, unshaven, with his clothes in tatters, and smelling of pigs, he considers that he is no more worthy to be called his father's son. The wonder of this parable is that his father had been looking out for him all the time; He saw him coming from a great way off and ran to greet his son with hugs and kisses, this despite his son's filthy state and the overwhelming smell of pigs which hung all over him.

The moral of the parable appears to be that it does not matter what sins we have committed, or indeed what state we are in, there is always a way back to the Father for the repentant sinner, as Jesus Christ (Yeshua Messiah) has paid the price for our sins on the cross. The apostle Paul makes this very clear, as he states:

> "***But God demonstrates His own love toward us, in that while we were still sinners, Christ died for us.***"
> (Romans 5:8, NKJV)

An obvious connection with the Prodigal son is found in the Parable of the Lost Sheep which Yeshua relates in the same chapter, as He addresses a great crowd of tax collectors and sinners in the book of Luke:

> "4 ***What man of you, having a hundred sheep, if he loses one of them, does he not leave the ninety-nine in the wilderness, and go after the one which is lost until he finds it?*** 5 ***And when he has found it, he lays it on his shoulders, rejoicing.*** 6 ***And when he comes home, he calls to his friends and neighbors,***

> *saying to them, 'Rejoice with me, for I have found my sheep which was lost!'* 7 *I say to you that likewise there will be more joy in heaven over one sinner who repents than over ninety-nine just persons who need no repentance."*
> (Luke 15:4-7, NKJV)

It appears from the above verses that the core message of the parable is that there is always a way back for the sinner who is lost, and that the way back to the Father's house is through repentance and an absolute belief in the saving sacrifice of Jesus Christ on the cross. The truth is that we are "**saved by grace**." It is also true that we are saved by grace because we have "**repented**." Clearly, this is a most important revelation of the Father's heart, which rings absolutely true. The question I want to pose here is this, is this *really* all Yeshua meant to convey to His disciples?

The question we need to ask ourselves is, what if there is still more to this parable than we understand on the surface? Might there be yet another message hidden from our view?

What else did Yeshua really intend to convey to His disciples? Let's look at it again as it might just be terribly important. What was really on His heart when He told them this parable? To get to the full meaning Yeshua meant to convey, we will need to adopt a Hebrew mindset as we re-examine the parable.

What was on Yeshua's mind when He gave this parable?

One of the most remarkable and frequently overlooked facts about the parables is the revelation that Yeshua spoke in parables in order to hide the truth. It is not generally understood that the reason our Messiah spoke in parables was because the message He really wanted to convey was not intended for general consumption. Once we truly understand this aspect, we will never look at any of His parables in the same light again. To discover the full meaning of the parable, we need to discover what was on Yeshua's mind when He gave this parable to His disciples. Yeshua spoke in parables in order to hide the truth. This seems incredible to most believers but our Messiah nevertheless made it very clear, as speaking to His disciples He said:

> "9 *Then His disciples asked Him, saying, "What does this parable mean?"* 10 *And He said, "To you it has been given to know the mysteries of the kingdom of God, but to the rest it is given in parables, that:* **'Seeing they may not see, And hearing they may not understand.'**""
>
> (Luke 8:9-10, emphasis added, NKJV)

> "10 **But when He was alone, those around Him with the twelve asked Him about the parable.** 11 **And He said to them, "To you it has been given to know the MYSTERY of the**

> ***kingdom of God; but to those who are outside, all things come in parables,*** ¹² ***so that…*** ***'Seeing they may see and not perceive, And hearing they may hear and not understand; Lest they should turn, And their sins be forgiven them.' "*** ¹³ ***And He said to them, "Do you not understand this parable? How then will you understand all the parables?"***
>
> (Mark 4:10-13, emphasis added, NKJV)

In view of the above, it is more than probable that Yeshua was addressing a subject that was only familiar to His inner circle. It was only His close disciples who were given to understand the *'mysteries of the Kingdom of God.'* In this term, we are given a vital clue, as this parable much like most of His other parables were related to the Kingdom of God.

We can find out quite a lot about what was most important to Yeshua's mind, by examining the Gospel He preached:

> "***And Jesus*** (Yeshua) ***went about all Galilee, teaching in their synagogues, preaching the GOSPEL OF THE KINGDOM,***"
>
> (Matthew 4:23, comment and emphasis added, NKJV)

Yeshua also showed us where His heart truly was when He gave us His model prayer:

> "9 **After this manner therefore pray ye: Our Father which art in heaven, Hallowed be thy name.** 10 **THY KINGDOM COME. Thy will be done in earth, as it is in heaven**."
> (Matthew 6:9-10, emphasis added, KJV)

What is this Kingdom Yeshua speaks of? The Kingdom He is referring to is none other than the United Kingdom of Israel over which He is destined to rule as King of Kings and Lord of Lords. It is only when His Kingdom is established upon the earth that the Father's will, will finally be done on earth as it is in heaven! What we need to understand is that this Kingdom is Israel! YHVH, the GOD of ISRAEL'S Divine plan calls for the restoration of the Whole House of Israel which is the desire of our Messiah's heart.

This is confirmed by Yeshua's exhortation to His disciples in Matthew 6:33 where He said: *"But seek ye first THE KINGDOM OF GOD!"*

The Apostle Paul too: *"...solemnly testified of the kingdom of God,"* and as he dwelt in his rented house in Rome, he received all who came to him: *"Preaching the kingdom of God"* (Acts 28:23 and 31, NKJV) As Paul was preaching about the kingdom of God, he was in effect proclaiming the messianic vision of the Restoration of the Kingdom of Israel.

Therefore, the hidden meaning of the parable can only be revealed to those who have that same Messianic

Hebrew vision of the restoration of the Kingdom of God. Furthermore, the mysteries of the Kingdom of God can be opened up only to those who have a Hebrew mindset. This mindset can only be acquired by obtaining a good knowledge of the history of Israel, and for this, we need to study Israel's history book.

The Bible is Israel's history book

Most believers accept that the Bible is a revelation about the Creator God, which has become the foundation for the beliefs of the two major monotheistic religions of the world that recognize the God of Israel: Judaism and Christianity. What is not generally appreciated is that the Bible, at the same time, is also the most accurate and unbiased history book in the world. In its pages, we find a record of the history of only one nation and people. Maybe, you have not thought of it in this way before, but Israel is the central focus of the Scriptures, and it is around this one nation and people that absolutely everything in its text revolves. Other nations or peoples mentioned in the Bible only feature as they come into contact with Israel. Thus, the Bible can well and truly be called *Israel's History Book*. The Scripture refers to the nation of Israel some 2,583 times. This alone demonstrates the paramount importance God attaches to His chosen nation.

The Church has an unfortunate history of replacement theology going back for nearly 2,000 years which has marginalized the central importance of Israel. The place of God's chosen nation has thus been sidelined, if not edited out of the picture altogether. Nevertheless, Israel is what the Bible is all about, and if we are to understand the Word of God, or indeed the parables of Yeshua, His only begotten Son, then we need to look at them through the prism of Israel.

This also means that if we really are seekers after truth, then we need to become familiar with the whole book, and not just devote our time to the New Testament alone. Most Bible scholars will readily accept that the New Testament cannot be understood without a thorough knowledge of the Old Testament. It follows therefore that the Parables of Yeshua can never reveal their hidden meaning regarding the '*Mysteries of the Kingdom of God*' without us having at the same time a comprehensive knowledge of the history of Israel which is found in the Old Testament.

Be Seekers After Truth!

Israel is the apple of God's eye

We need to be mindful that our Father in Heaven refers to Himself as the God of Israel.

> *"Then you shall say to Pharaoh, 'Thus says the LORD: "Israel is My son, My firstborn."*
> (Exodus 4:22, NKJV)

Our Almighty Creator God thus identifies Himself as the Father of Israel, and in speaking to Moses on Mount Sinai, He said:

> "5 **Now therefore, if you will indeed obey My voice and keep My covenant, then you shall be a special treasure to Me above all people; for all the earth is Mine.** 6 **And you shall be to Me a kingdom of priests and a holy nation. These are the words which you shall speak to the children of Israel**."
> (Exodus 19:5-6, NKJV)

This is a foundational Scripture as Israel's ultimate destiny is to become a kingdom of priests and a holy nation. In this, we are given a prophecy of the Messianic Kingdom that is to come at a yet future time when Israel's destiny is fulfilled. The Gospel of the Kingdom which Yeshua and His disciples, including the Apostle Paul, preached was essentially about the establishment of this same Kingdom.

The divine covenant the Bible speaks of is made with only one nation...

> "*...I have made a covenant with you and with Israel.*"
> (Exodus 34:27, NKJV)

After Moses was given the text for the Aaronic blessing by the Almighty Elohim, he was given the concluding verse as follows:

> "*So they shall put My name on the children of Israel, and I will bless them.*"
> (Numbers 6:27, NKJV)

Thus, the Creator of the Universe and Author of All Life has placed His Eternal Name upon His chosen people Israel. Thus, YHVH the Elohim of Israel made an irreversible decision that can never be changed, as He stated:

> "*For I am the LORD, I do not change!*"
> (Malachi 3:6, NKJV)

King David in his Psalms frequently refers to God as 'The Holy One of Israel.'

> "*...To You I will sing with the harp, O Holy One of Israel.*"
> (Psalms 71:22, NKJV)

One of the most amazing divine declarations of God's love for his people is made by Moses in his final words to the children of Israel just prior to his death:

> "9 **For the LORD'S portion is His people; Jacob is the place of His**

> *inheritance. ⁱ⁰ He found him in a desert land And in the wasteland, a howling wilderness; He encircled him, He instructed him, He kept him as the apple of His eye.*"
> (Deuteronomy 32:9-10, NKJV)

When we look at all of this scriptural evidence, we can see that God's heart is focused on His people, the children of Israel. Israel is His nation! The Israelites and **all their descendants** are His chosen people. Everything God does and whatever He speaks has therefore to be seen in the light of Israel. The same goes for Messiah Yeshua, His only begotten Son. Yeshua does not have a different approach to His Father, as He made the following statements to His disciples:

> "⁹ *...He who has seen Me has seen the Father; so how can you say 'Show us the Father'?* ¹⁰ *Do you not believe that I am in the Father, and the Father in Me? The words that I speak to you I do not speak on My own authority; but the Father who dwells in Me does the works*."
> (John 14:9b-10, NKJV)

> "*But that the world may know that I love the Father, and as the Father gave Me commandment, so do I...*"
> (John 14:31, NKJV)

Thus, if the Father's love and concern is wholly focused upon His chosen nation Israel, we can expect His Son to have the same overriding concern. In this, we are given a vital key in unlocking the *Mystery of the Kingdom of God*, whose secret code Yeshua hid in His parables. This *key* is the realization that the parables are essentially about Israel and her future destiny. The primary purpose of the parables therefore is not to convey some moral lesson or truth, although most of them do so, but rather to give a prophecy about Israel's future restoration.

Who is the father of the Prodigal Son?

The first thing we need to realize is that this parable is about Israel. The father being spoken of is none other than God the Father, the Holy One of Israel. Remember, Israel is His firstborn son whose destiny it is to become a Kingdom of priests and a holy nation. He has made a covenant with her and placed His Name upon her, and she is the apple of His eye.

A terrible breach has occurred

Sadly, a spirit of rebellion has taken hold of His people and consequently a terrible breach has taken place. His nation Israel, which was comprised of twelve tribes, became a divided kingdom. The breach

occurred after the reign of King Solomon, when the ten tribes of northern Israel rebelled against the divine order, to set up their own kingdom to the north of Jerusalem. The rump of the original kingdom was centered on Jerusalem and it took the name of Judah after its leading tribe, whereas the ten tribes, which seceded from the House of David, applied the name Israel with Samaria as their new capital. We thus see Israel divided into two kingdoms, one called Judah and the other Israel. This sad divorce between the tribes of Israel has been faithfully recorded for us in 1 Kings 12:1-33. Ever since that time, the Bible, Israel's history book, has referred to the former United Davidic Kingdom of Israel, as the Kingdom/House of Judah, and the Kingdom or House of Israel, with each nation following its own path. They have remained totally separate entities ever since the division occurred some three thousand years ago. When we understand this historic fact we have uncovered one of the most important keys to understanding the prophecies of the Bible.

Who are those two sons of the father in this parable?

It is only as we understand what happened to Israel way back then that we can begin to comprehend what Yeshua was getting at when He referred to a father with two sons. Remember, He is the Father of Israel as Israel is His firstborn son (Exodus 4:22). The father in the parable therefore is none other than God the Father, the Holy One of Israel. Thus, when Israel divides into two kingdoms, the Father acquires two sons, and it is these two sons, one called Judah and the other called Israel, who now represents the new reality. The allegorical interpretation is that of a father who had two sons, e.g. one representing the unfaithful/prodigal House of Israel and the other the faithful House of Judah, as only Judah, as represented by the Jewish people, has largely remained faithful to the Torah, the instructions of the Holy One of Israel. The ten tribes of the House of Israel on the other hand broke their covenant with YHVH, the God of Israel and went headlong into paganism and idolatry.

Are they mentioned elsewhere in the Bible?

Yes, hundreds of times, especially in the prophets! Furthermore, the separation between the House of Judah and the House of Israel is amply recorded both in the historical books of Kings and Chronicles. This tragic divorce occurred in the first year of the reign of King Rehoboam, who succeeded his father Solomon in 930 B.C. Thus, over three thousand years ago, Israel was split into two kingdoms. You can read all about it in Israel's history book in 1 Kings, the 11th and 12th chapters. Ever since that day, the books of Kings and Chronicles have recorded the separate histories of the two kingdoms including the kings list of the respective royal dynasties ruling over them. The Bible also records several occasions when Judah and Israel go to war against each other. In one such incident the Scriptures even speak of a king of Israel taking the king of Judah captive and sacking Jerusalem! Israel's history book records the event as follows:

> "**¹¹ But Amaziah would not heed. Therefore Jehoash king of Israel went out; so he and Amaziah king of Judah faced one another at Beth Shemesh, which belongs to Judah. ¹² And Judah was defeated by Israel, and every man fled to his tent. ¹³ Then Jehoash king of Israel captured Amaziah king of Judah, the son of Jehoash, the son of Ahaziah, at Beth Shemesh; and he went to Jerusalem, and broke down the wall of Jerusalem from the Gate of Ephraim to the Corner gate—four hundred cubits. ¹⁴ And he took all the gold and silver, all the articles that were found in the house of the LORD and in the treasuries of the king's house, and hostages, and returned to Samaria.**"
>
> (2 Kings 14:11-14, NKJV)

Ever since the separation occurred, the prophets of Israel have been speaking of the day when the two nations will come together again. '**THE**' major prophetic theme of the prophets of the Bible is the ultimate restoration of the two houses of Israel into one United Kingdom. Even the apostle Peter referred to this restoration when he addressed his countrymen from the house of Judah in Solomon's Porch:

> "*19* ***Repent ye therefore, and be converted, that your sins may be blotted out, when the times of refreshing shall come from the presence of the LORD;*** *20* ***And he shall send Jesus Christ*** (Yeshua Messiah)***, which before was preached unto you:*** *21* ***Whom the heaven must receive until the times of restitution of all things which God hath spoken by the mouth of all his holy prophets since the world began.***"
> (Acts 3:19-21, comment added, KJV)

Restitution means restoring to a former state or condition and it is speaking here about the restoration of God's government on the earth through His nation Israel. Peter goes on in verse 22 to refer to the words of Moses who spoke about the Messiah to come as follows:

> "***The LORD your God will raise up for you a Prophet like me from your midst, from your brethren. Him you shall hear,***"
> (Deuteronomy 18:15, NKJV)

To summarize, Judah and Israel, the two sons of the Father, are most certainly mentioned in the Bible, and it may well be said that the whole of God's Word revolves around those two.

What is meant by the father's house and where is its location?

The father's house is a reference to the Land of Israel. As the Scripture says:

> *"The land shall not be sold permanently, for the land is Mine; for you are strangers and sojourners with Me."*
> (Leviticus 25:23, NKJV)

It is also in the Land of Israel where King Solomon was commissioned by the God of Israel to build the Temple of the LORD:

> "*1 And it came to pass, when Solomon had finished building the house of the LORD……… 2 that the LORD appeared to Solomon the second time, as He had appeared to him at Gibeon. 3 And the LORD said to him: "I have heard your prayer and your supplication that you have made before Me; I have consecrated this house which you have built to put My NAME there forever, and My eyes and My heart will be there perpetually*."
> (1 Kings 9:1-3, emphasis added, NKJV)

The father's house clearly is in the place where the Eternal Father of Israel placed His Name and where He had His house. Thus, in using the term the '*house of the father*' in the parable, Messiah Yeshua is speaking about the Land of Israel. In fact, the little strip of land on the Mediterranean coast presently occupied by the State of Israel is as nothing to the land God promised to Abraham by an eternal covenant.

> ***"On the same day the LORD made a covenant with Abram, saying: "To your descendants I have given this land, from the river of Egypt to the great river, the River Euphrates—""***
> (Genesis 15:18, NKJV)

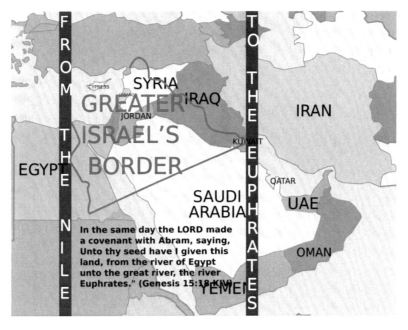

In the days of King Solomon, this promise had its initial fulfilment, as the writ of Solomon stretched all the way from the River Nile in Egypt to the River Euphrates in present day Iraq. During his reign, Israel experienced forty years of peace and a time of exceptional prosperity. The Sages of Israel consider his reign to have been but a small foretaste of the millennial era that is to be ushered in by the Messiah of Israel. All of this extra land promised to the descendants of Abraham will surely be needed when the prodigal ten tribes of Israel return to the Father's house to join their brother Judah.

Why does the Prodigal son leave his father's house?

It was his rebellion against the covenant which caused prodigal Israel to be expelled from the land. Subsequent to their separation from Judah, the ten seceding tribes of Israel, led by the tribe of Ephraim, departed from the Torah. Their king, Jeroboam, set up golden calves for his people to worship and led the nation headlong into idolatry and hedonistic materialism. In His love for His chosen people, God sent many prophets to warn them of the consequences of their sins, yet all to no avail, as the rebellious House of Israel refused to heed the multiple warnings given to them. Those prophets over and again listed all the curses for disobedience enumerated by Moses in the book of Deuteronomy, but Israel simply would not listen.

> "45 **Moreover all these curses shall come upon you and pursue and overtake you, until you are destroyed, because you did not obey the voice of the LORD your**

> *God, to keep His commandments and His statutes which He commanded you.* [46] *And they shall be upon you for a sign and a wonder, and on your descendants forever.* [47] *Because you did not serve the LORD your God with joy and gladness of heart, for the abundance of everything,* [48] *therefore you shall serve your enemies, whom the LORD will send against you, in hunger, in thirst, in nakedness, and in need of everything; and He will put a yoke of iron on your neck until He has destroyed you.* [49] *The LORD will bring a nation against you from afar, from the end of the earth, as swift as the eagle flies, a nation whose language you will not understand,* [50] *a nation of fierce countenance, which does not respect the elderly nor show favor to the young.*"
> (Deuteronomy 28:45-50, NKJV)

Moses words and the stark prophetic warnings they contained eventually came to pass as the fearful Assyrian Empire assailed the Kingdom of Israel in three successive invasions. Each time a large section of the Israelite population was taken away and deported to the northern most reaches of their empire. The final deportation took place at the end of a three years' siege of the capital city of Samaria in 721 B.C.

Thus, the ultimate sanction for disobedience which Moses had outlined to the children of Israel finally came into effect after they had rejected and ignored all the warnings of the prophets of Israel for nearly 200 years.

> "⁶³ **And it shall be, that just as the LORD rejoiced over you to do you good and multiply you, so the LORD will rejoice over you to destroy you and bring you to nothing; and you shall be plucked from off the land which you go to possess.** ⁶⁴ **Then the LORD will scatter you among all the peoples, from one end of the earth to the other, and there you shall serve other gods,…"**
> (Deuteronomy 28:63-64, NKJV)

This is how the Prodigal House of Israel ended up in a far country miles away from his Father's house, where he wasted his spiritual inheritance with prodigal living. Judah was the older son of the father in the Parable whereas, Israel, who was led by Ephraim, the younger son of Joseph, was the younger son who left his father's house. The truth is that ever since the two houses of Israel have been apart, it has been the Father's intention one day to bring the two houses together into one nation and One Kingdom once again. This is essentially what the Gospel of the Kingdom is all about, as the Father's heart of the God of Israel yearns for the time when His nation is restored into One United Kingdom once again. In this parable, Yeshua is prophesying that the ten northern tribes of Israel which were taken into captivity by the Assyrians in 721 B.C. will one day return to their ancestral home in the land of Israel.

Why does the prodigal son leave his father's house? Well, the answer is that it was his spirit of rebellion and his involvement into the occult that caused him to be removed by force. The prodigal son was simply reaping what he had sown and he was expelled from the Land and scattered among the nations even to the ends of the earth (Deuteronomy 28:64).

What do the pigs signify?

Every word of Messiah Yeshua in this parable has a deep significance, and so it is with the pigs. The prodigal son ended up in a faraway land where he was forced to tend to another man's pigs. What possibly can this mean? The Word of God always interprets itself and we find the answer in the Scriptures:

> "**[1] Now the LORD spoke to Moses and Aaron, saying to them, [2] "Speak to the children of Israel, saying, 'These are the animals which you may eat among all the animals that are on the earth: [3] Among the animals, whatever**

> ***divides the hoof, having cloven hooves and chewing the cud—that you may eat,*** ... [7] ***and the swine, though it divides the hoof, having cloven hooves, yet does not chew the cud, is unclean to you.*** [8] ***Their flesh you shall not eat, and their carcasses you shall not touch. They are unclean to you.'***"
> (Leviticus 11:1-3, 7-8, NKJV)

In the previous chapter, we find a most significant statement which puts the above divine health law in perfect context:

> "[10] ***That you may distinguish between holy and unholy, and between unclean and clean,*** [11] ***and that you may teach the children of Israel all the statutes which the LORD has spoken to them by the hand of Moses.***"
> (Leviticus 10:10-11, NKJV)

A thousand years before Moses, Noah was asked to take seven clean animals and only two unclean animals on board the ark:

> "***You shall take with you seven each of every clean animal, a male and his female; two each of animals that are unclean, a male and his female;***"
> (Genesis 7:2, NKJV)

Clearly, Noah was well aware of *which* animals God had declared fit for human consumption and which were not suitable for food. This puts one in mind of the time when our Creator used to instruct our ancestors Adam and Eve in the Garden of Eden, as the knowledge of what animals were clean and which were not must have been handed down through the generations from Adam to Noah.

So, what then is the connection with the prodigal son having to work with pigs? The link is simply that the pigs are unclean and unclean stands for unholy. The prodigal house of Israel was thrust out of his ancestral land because of his unclean and unholy behaviour having forsaken the Law of Moses and rebelled against His Father, the Holy One of Israel. This also, rather, sums up the condition of the Church at large, which teaches that God's Law has been done away with and that Yeshua has nailed it to the cross. If this were true, then it would have been an act of gross insubordination, as Yeshua has no authority to change the Law of His Father, and He most certainly never would! One can deduce this from the following foundational passage:

> "[1] **In the beginning was the Word** [Torah]**, and the Word was with God, and the Word was God**... [14] **And the Word** [Torah] **became flesh and dwelt** [tabernacled] **among us, and we beheld His glory, the glory as of the only begotten of the Father, full of grace and truth**."
> (John 1:1 & 14, comments added, NKJV)

Yeshua is the Word [Torah] made flesh! Anyone who says that any portion of the Torah (the Word) is "*done away with*" is saying that Yeshua is done away with. The truth is that our Saviour was most emphatic about His respect for His Fathers Law, as He said:

> **"Do not think that I came to destroy the Law or the Prophets. I did not come to destroy but to fulfill."**
> (Matthew 5:17, NKJV)

The word "*fulfill*" here does not mean cancel, rather it means that He has come to bring the Law/Torah of His Father to its fullest expression. His purpose was to bring it to its completion, by making it possible for us to obey the '*spirit of the Law*' through the gift of the Holy Spirit. Yeshua came to magnify the Law and show us that sin starts in the mind; that even if I think anger, I have already killed my brother; if even I think lust; I have already committed adultery, so that no man can stand justified before the Father by the works of the Law alone. We need to also take into account that the Spirit of God will never contradict the Written Word of God, or indeed the word of Yeshua, our Messiah, and Redeemer, or else, it is a different spirit.

The prodigal son made a life choice, and much like the famous song immortalized by Frank Sinatra; "*I did it My way,*" he walked in disobedience to His Father. He was not prepared to live by God's standards which, had he done so, would have brought him countless blessings. When a man goes against God's standards of righteousness, he is likened to a man walking in the face of a mighty wind. But when one repents, he changes direction and goes with the wind that was at one time against him. The Holy One of Israel does not change His standards of righteousness, His Torah endures forever. Where we stand in relation to it will determine what happens to us. The Prodigal Son rejected the holy for the unholy and the clean for the unclean, and this is why he came to endure the mighty famine, which brings us full circle back to why he ended up with the pigs.

What about the mighty famine, what does it mean?

What about the mighty famine that arose in the land of his exile? Remember, it was the mighty famine which brought the Prodigal Son finally to his senses. Until it happened, he seemed oblivious to his true condition. It took the famine to make him aware. This famine Yeshua speaks of in His parable is an allegorical reference to the period the Bible speaks of as the "***time of Jacob's trouble***," which is designed to bring the Lost House of Israel, e.g. the Prodigal Son to repentance. The *'Time of Jacob's Trouble'* is a time of unprecedented calamity which is prophesied to befall all the 12 tribal sons of Jacob including Judah. It is the same time Yeshua describes as the *'Great Tribulation'* as recorded in Matthew 24, Mark 13 and Luke 21.

The prophet Jeremiah speaks most eloquently about this time at the end of the age:

"3 ***'For behold, the days are coming,'*** ***says the LORD, 'that I will bring back***

> *from captivity My people Israel and Judah,' says the LORD. 'And I will cause them to return to the land that I gave to their fathers, and they shall possess it.'* 4 *Now these are the words that the LORD spoke concerning ISRAEL and JUDAH."*
>
> (Jeremiah 30:3-4, emphasis added, NKJV)

Notice that Jeremiah is addressing his prophecy to the two distinct sons of the Father, e.g. Israel and Judah! The promise is that the eternal God of Israel is going to bring them both back from captivity (Ezekiel 28:25). We know that God the Father has already started this process, as around 40% of those who are known to be of Jewish stock have already returned to the Land ever since the establishment of the State of Israel in 1948. It took a holocaust to bring most of them back to the Land and the prophecy indicates that it will take another holocaust, this time not for the Jews alone, but for all the Israelite sons of Jacob. The irony is that most of them are not even aware of their Israelite ancestry. The time will come; perhaps we are even now on the threshold of that time, when the whole world will know who and where those missing Israelites are. Jeremiah predicts that their journey back to the land of their fathers is a time of great calamity and tribulation:

> "5 *For thus says the LORD: 'We have heard a voice of trembling, of fear, and not of peace.* 6 *Ask now, and see, whether a man is even in labor with child; So why do I see every*

> *man with his hands on his loins like a woman in labor, and all faces pale? 7 Alas! For that day is great, So that none is like it; And it is the time of Jacob's trouble, but he shall be saved out of it. 8 'For it shall come to pass in that day,' says the LORD of hosts, 'That I will break the yoke from your neck, And will burst your bonds; foreigners shall no more enslave them. 9 But they shall serve the LORD their God, and David their king, whom I will raise up for them."*
>
> (Jeremiah 30:5-9, NKJV)

Just as the great famine motivated the prodigal son to re-examine his life and situation, so it will also be when the '*Time of Jacob's Trouble*' hits home to those of the Lost House of Israel. Just as the prodigal son lost his prosperity and became totally destitute, so are the people who comprise the ten tribes of Israel destined to suffer the same fate. At the end of the day, their only hope of survival will be to return to the Father's house, e.g. the Land of Israel. They will be a greatly chastened band of returnees. Buffeted as they have by the terrors and terrible trials of the '*Great Tribulation*,' their journey will be a journey of learning as well as return. As they set out on their long journey home; hungry, unwashed, unshaven, with their clothes in tatters, and smelling of pigs, which represents their unclean and unholy lifestyle, they too, like the prodigal son, consider that they are no more worthy to be called their Father's son.

Why is the prodigal son given a new robe by his Father?

As they approach the Land, they too will discover that their Father has been looking out for them all the time, as He sees them coming from a great way off, He will run to greet them with hugs and kisses all-round, this despite their filthy state and the overwhelming smell of pigs which hangs all over them. They will come in a great throng weeping, ready to confess their sins with their eyes full of tears of repentance having come through the manifold tribulations of the *'Time of Jacob's Trouble.'* The Prophet Jeremiah puts it very well:

> "*16* **Thus says the LORD: "Refrain your voice from weeping, and your eyes from tears; For your work shall be rewarded, says the LORD, and they shall come back from the land of the enemy.** *17* **There is hope in your future, says the LORD, That your children shall come back to their own border.**"
>
> (Jeremiah 31:16-17, NKJV)

Israel/Ephraim then confesses how he feels greatly humbled and ashamed. He can literally kick himself for what he has done, and the Prophet Jeremiah movingly records Ephraim's sentiment in the next passage:

> "**[18] I have surely heard Ephraim** (the House of Israel) **bemoaning himself; 'You have chastised me, and I was chastised, like an untrained bull; Restore me, and I will return, For You are the LORD my God. [19] Surely, after my turning, I repented; And after I was instructed, I struck myself on the thigh; I was ashamed, yes, even humiliated, Because I bore the reproach of my youth.'"**
> (Jeremiah 31:18-19, comment added, NKJV)

Notice, it was after they were '*instructed*,' that they struck themselves on the thigh and became utterly ashamed. The Hebrew word '*Torah*' is generally translated as *Law* in most English translations, yet, the *true meaning* of Torah is *instruction*!

The Torah is God's instruction in righteousness.

The Torah is God's instruction in righteousness; it is the teaching that reflects God's own standards. After Ephraim's return, he is going to be instructed all over again, as he needs to undergo a process of re-education. As he discovers more and more what God's standards really are, he will become terribly ashamed of his former lifestyle, and he strikes

Tallit (Prayer Shawl)

himself on the thigh. He literally wants to kick himself for not having lived that way, and consequently having missed out on all the blessings that would have flowed from his obedience to the Torah, the instructions of His Father in Heaven.

So, what of the robe? Well, it is at this point the Father orders His servants to bring forth the Best Robe, and put it on him. The Robe means that the Prodigal Son from here on is going to be clothed in the Torah—the Living Word. The Robe is in fact the Tallit, (the Jewish prayer shawl), which together with its four fringes (tzitzits), symbolizes all 613 commandments of the Torah. It is the same robe the Prophet Isaiah speaks of:

> ***"I will greatly rejoice in the LORD, My soul shall be joyful in my God; For He has clothed me with the garments of salvation, He has covered me with the robe of righteousness. As a bridegroom decks himself with ornaments, and as a bride adorns herself with her jewels."***
> (Isaiah 61:10, NKJV)

Being clothed with *"the garments of salvation"* is to be clothed with the garments of Yeshua, whose Hebrew name signifies salvation. Filled with joy at the return of Ephraim (the Lost House of Israel) the Father clothes His long lost children in Yeshua's Robe of Righteousness. The Father is filled with joy because now the process of reconciliation between the two estranged houses of Israel, which have been apart for three thousand years, can finally begin.

Why does the father place a ring on the prodigal's hand?

Yes, indeed what of the ring? Why does the father command his servants to put a ring on his hand? The ring is symbolically very important, as it signifies authority. It was a *sign* of his high position in the family. The ring is a crested signet ring like the one on the right, representative of the Father's own authority. By placing this ring on the prodigal son's hand, the Father is acknowledging Ephraim as His firstborn son. The Prophet Jeremiah once again provides confirmation for this:

> "*...For I am a Father to Israel, and Ephraim is MY firstborn.*"
> (Jeremiah 31:9b, NKJV)

King David also refers to Ephraim's exalted position in the Father's house:

> "*...Ephraim also is the helmet for My head; Judah is My lawgiver.*"
> (Psalms 60:7b, NKJV)

Ephraim's helmet is also referred to by the Apostle Paul, as he urges the true disciples of Yeshua to put on the whole armour of God:

> *"And take the helmet of salvation, and the sword of the Spirit, which is the word of God."*
> (Ephesians 6:17, NKJV)

Jeremiah gives a further moving passage in which the Father expresses His heart's concern about Ephraim:

> *"Is Ephraim My dear son? Is he a pleasant child? For though I spoke against him,* [in the Time of Jacob's Trouble] *I earnestly remember him still; Therefore My heart yearns for him; I will surely have mercy on him, says the LORD."*
> (Jeremiah 31:20, comment added, NKJV)

The Scriptures also provide a precedent for the signet ring of authority being given to Ephraim, as Ephraim is the descendant of Joseph to whom was given the blessing of the birthright.

> *"11 And Israel said to Joseph, "I had not thought to see your face; but in fact, God has also shown me your offspring!" 12 So Joseph brought them from beside his knees, and he bowed down with his face to the earth. 13 And Joseph took them both, Ephraim with his right hand toward Israel's left hand, and Manasseh with his left hand toward Israel's right hand, and brought them near him. 14 Then*

Israel stretched out his right hand and laid it on Ephraim's head, who was the younger, and his left hand on Manasseh's head, guiding his hands knowingly, for Manasseh was the firstborn. [15] *And he blessed Joseph, and said: "God, before whom my fathers Abraham and Isaac walked, The God who has fed me all my life long to this day,* [16] *The Angel who has redeemed me from all evil, Bless the lads; Let my name be named upon them, And the name of my fathers Abraham and Isaac; And let them grow into a multitude in the midst of the earth."* [17] *Now when Joseph saw that his father laid his right hand on the head of Ephraim, it displeased him; so he took hold of his father's hand to remove it from Ephraim's head to Manasseh's head.* [18] *And Joseph said to his father, "Not so, my father, for this one is the firstborn; put your right hand on his head."* [19] *But his father refused and said, "I know, my son, I know. He also shall become a people, and he also shall be great; but truly his younger brother shall be greater than he, and his descendants shall become a multitude of nations."* [20]

So he blessed them that day, saying, "By you Israel will bless, saying, 'May God make you as Ephraim and as Manasseh!'" And thus he set Ephraim before Manasseh."

(Genesis 48:11-20, NKJV)

"22 Joseph is a fruitful bough, A fruitful bough by a well; His branches run over the wall. 23 The archers have bitterly grieved him, Shot at him and hated him. 24 But his bow remained in strength, And the arms of his hands were made strong By the hands of the Mighty God of Jacob (From there is the Shepherd, the Stone of Israel), 25 By the God of your father who will help you, And by the Almighty who will bless you With blessings of heaven above, Blessings of the deep that lies beneath, Blessings of the breasts and of the womb. 26 The blessings of your father Have excelled the blessings of my ancestors, Up to the utmost bound of the everlasting hills. They shall be on the head of Joseph, And on the crown of the head of him who was separate from his brothers."

(Genesis 49:22-26, NKJV)

The account of Joseph, the ancestor of Ephraim, receiving his seal of authority from Pharaoh is given as follows:

> "⁴¹ **And Pharaoh said to Joseph, "See, I have set you over all the land of Egypt."** ⁴² **Then Pharaoh took his signet ring of his hand; and put it on Joseph's hand; and he clothed him in garments of fine linen and put a gold chain around his neck**."
> (Genesis 41:41-42, NKJV)

What is the significance of the sandals placed on his feet?

So, what of the sandals? The sandals showed that he was a son instead of a slave, since slaves did not usually wear sandals as they went about barefoot. Yet the sandals serve a much greater purpose than this, as is made clear by the Apostle Paul:

> "**And having shod your feet with the preparation of the gospel of peace;**"
> (Ephesians 6:15, NKJV)

This gospel of peace is none other than the Gospel of the Kingdom which Yeshua and His Apostles preached. It is only when our King Messiah, the King of Peace, rules over the restored and reunited Kingdom of Israel that the world will finally come to know the meaning of true peace. The Apostle Paul is reflecting the very heart of Our Father in Heaven as he addresses the early believers in Rome, by saying:

> ***"Brethren, my heart's desire and prayer to God for Israel is that they may be saved."***
> (Romans 10:1, NKJV)

> "***26 And so all Israel*** (both Houses) ***will be saved, as it is written: "The Deliverer will come out of Zion, And He will turn away ungodliness from Jacob;*** 27 ***For this is My covenant with them, When I take away their sins."***
> (Romans 11:26-27, comment added, NKJV)

When the prodigal House of Israel returns to the Land of the Father with their hearts full of repentance, they will have their feet shod with the Gospel of Peace. In their subsequent walk, as they wear Yeshua's Garment of Salvation and His Robe of Righteousness, they cannot but exude a powerful example in the house of their Father (the Land of Israel). The Apostle Paul again sums it up in the most beautiful way:

> ***"And how shall they preach unless they are sent? As it is written: "How beautiful are the feet of those who preach the gospel of peace, Who bring glad tidings of good things!"***
> (Romans 10:15, NKJV)

Why the fatted calf and the great feast?

Imagine what a celebration there will be, both in heaven and in all the earth, when both the Houses of Judah and Israel become One again, having been separated for 3,000 long years? It will be the mother of all celebrations! Can you imagine what a party that will be when finally Messiah, the Son of David, rules over the REUNITED KINGDOM OF ISRAEL? In the Book of Revelation this feast is described as the marriage of the Lamb:

> ***"Let us be glad and rejoice and give Him glory, for the marriage of the Lamb has come, and His wife*** (The Whole House of Israel) ***has made herself ready."***
> (Revelation 19:7, comment added, NKJV)

Why is the older brother angry?

Why was Judah angry when his younger brother returns to his father's house? Remember, how in the parable the older brother was angry and would not go in to the party to welcome his long lost brother! Why was he angry? What was his beef? Well, to begin with he did not think his younger

Prodigal son's brother is angry and he will not join in the festivity

brother deserved to have a great feast, as he made his feelings quite clear to his father, who had come out and pleaded with him to join in the celebrations:

> "29 ***So he answered and said to his father, 'Lo, these many years I have been serving you; I never transgressed your commandment at any time; and yet you never gave me a young goat, that I might make merry with my friends.*** 30 ***But as soon as this son of yours came, who has devoured your livelihood with harlots; you killed the fatted calf for him.'***"
>
> (Luke 15:29-30, NKJV)

What lies behind the prodigal son's older brother's attitude? Why is he not pleased to see his long lost brother return to his father's house? Judah thought that his father was not being fair to him, but he also thought his father was being unjust. He reminded his father that, whilst he had always been an obedient and faithful son, he had never thrown a special party for him and his friends. He also pointed out that his prodigal brother hardly deserved this special treatment in that he had wasted his father's inheritance in cavorting with harlots. He really was quite upset and he would not go into the house to meet his brother; he simply could not bring himself to do it. He did not even want to meet his brother. In any case, if the truth be told; he had got quite used to being his father's only son.

Actually, Judah's attitude was anticipated by the Prophet Ezekiel. The Tanakh (O.T.) prophesied that this kind of reaction would occur. Ezekiel prophesied that in the end times, Judah would fear the return of his wayward brothers to the point where they will not want to receive them:

> "*15* ***Son of man, your brethren, your relatives, your countrymen, and all the house of Israel in its entirety, are those about whom the inhabitants of Jerusalem have said, 'Get far away from the LORD; this land has been given to us as a possession.'...*** *17* ***Therefore say, 'Thus says the LORD GOD: "I will gather you from the peoples, assemble you from the countries where you have been scattered, and I will give you the land of Israel." '...*** *19* ***"Then I will give them one heart, and I will put a new spirit within them, and take the stony heart out of their flesh, and give them a heart of flesh,*** *20* ***that they may walk in My statutes and keep My judgments and do them, and they shall be My people, and I will be their God." "***
> (Ezekiel 11:15, 17, 19-20, NKJV)

The rabbinic leaders of Judah are petrified at the prospect of millions of returning Christian Zionist and

Messianic believers from the ten tribes. Can we not understand their fears? They are afraid the Jewish society is going to be swamped by Christians with an evangelizing zeal to make converts of Jews. They are also most afraid of assimilation, as their sons and daughters are swept away in marriage to the newcomers. Notice, the prophecy is that they will be given the Land of Israel. Notice, it does not mention that they will be given the Land of Judah. In other words, those returning Israelites will be given the former territory of the Northern Kingdom of Israel to dwell in. This fact alone should make Judah feel somewhat better about the return of his long lost brothers.

Did the older son in the parable have a case?

Humanly speaking, the older son most certainly had a reason for being somewhat put out. After all, he was the one who had remained loyal to his father and served him all those years. The fact is that the Jewish people alone, (unlike their Israelite brethren of the Lost House of Israel), have borne the mantle of being God's *'chosen'* people, and consequently they have suffered much persecution. Throughout the history of the world, the Jews have been the most abused and kicked-around race of people on the earth. The truth is, that the world hates the *'Spiritual Realm of God,'* and this is why the world also hates the Jews. Man cannot stand the concept that the Jews are the *'chosen'* people of God.

The Israelites were chosen because they were the *'least'* of all people. Thus, they were not chosen because they were special; rather they have become special because they were chosen. That God should make a covenant with *'one'* people in itself is an affront to modern man. It is an affront to political correctness, but then the God of Israel does not play those foolish games. He is the Sovereign Author and Ruler of the Universe, and He chooses whoever He will. A popular Jewish saying goes: *"So, who asked to be chosen?"* It is true, they did not ask to be chosen, yet the Jewish people simply know from their four thousand years of experience that they are God's *'chosen'* people. The Jewish cynic will say: *"I wish God had chosen somebody else because it has brought us nothing but pain."* Whereas, it cannot be denied that it has brought them a lot of grief, but it has also given them many blessings and it is an awesome privilege and exceptional honour to be *'chosen'* of God. A most important point to remember here is that the Jews were not the only ones who were *'chosen'* by God by a special covenant. We must not forget that the ten tribes of Israel – those missing sons of Abraham – were also part of that same covenant even though they, unlike the Jews, failed to keep it.

The sole '*SIGN*' that identifies

Sadly, the Israelite nations are not aware of their true ancestry as the Lost House of Israel. They do not know *who* they are. They have *forgotten* their origins and they *think* of themselves as Gentiles when in truth, they are Israelites. They are *ignorant* of the fact and so is the rest of the world. The reason they have lost the knowledge of their ancient roots is because they departed from the God of Israel and, especially, because THEY LOST THE ONE "*SIGN*" THAT WOULD HAVE IDENTIFIED THEM! This *sign* is mentioned in the book of Exodus Chapter 31:

> "**12 And the LORD spoke to Moses, saying,** 13 **"Speak also to the children of Israel, saying: 'Surely My Sabbaths you shall keep, for it is a SIGN between Me and you throughout your generations, that you may know that I am the LORD who sanctifies you...'"** 17 **It is a SIGN between Me and the children of Israel forever; for in six days the LORD made the heavens and the earth, and on the seventh day He rested and was refreshed**."
> (Exodus 31:12-13 & 17, emphasis added, NKJV)

Here, we have the reason that the Israelite nations have lost the knowledge of *who* they are. They failed to keep God's seventh day Sabbaths, which was the One and Only Sign that would have identified them as God's chosen covenant people. At the same time, the Jewish people have never lost their identity as God's chosen people because, ever since they came out of their Babylonian captivity, they have been faithful to God's Sabbaths. Their seventh day Sabbath has become known in the world at large as *'the Jewish Sabbath.'* It is God's seventh day Sabbath that has more than anything else identified the Jews as *'God's chosen people'* and as *'the people of the Covenant.'* Being identified to the whole world by the *sign* of the Sabbath has come at a terrible price for the Jews. We can fairly say that, comparatively speaking, the members of the House of Israel had it easy compared to their brothers of the House of Judah, who being identified as God's chosen people have had it very hard indeed. The other tribes of Israel should have great respect for Judah, despite continual persecution, rejection and hardship, they have held to their *Torah*, that is to say the *'teaching and instructions'* of their God, regardless of all the suffering it has brought them.

What more can we learn about the older son who stays behind?

Although a number of Ephraimites and Messianic, as well as Christian Zionist believers in Messiah Yeshua have already settled in the Land of Israel, they are forced to live by faith, as the Jewish authorities in the State of Israel will generally only grant them three month visas. Most of them, believing it is the Father's will for them to be there, remain in the Land, and they will leave the Land briefly, only to re-enter the Land on a fresh three month visa. Currently the *"Right of Return"* only applies to those who can *prove* their Jewish origins, and those Ephraimites of the Lost House of Israel at the time of writing have no such right. This explains the reason why the other brother in the parable was not in any way looking out for his lost brother, as he was busy working in the field. Judah today is also not looking for his missing Israelite brothers. In fact, most Jews are completely unaware of their existence let alone their whereabouts. It must be said that among the Orthodox community, there are numerous rabbis and Torah scholars who are familiar with the words of the Prophets about the ultimate return of the Ten Tribes, and the promises of the Restoration of the United Kingdom of Israel. Ironically, the Sidur, the Jewish prayer book contains the Amidah prayer in which the observant Jews pray three times a day for the return of their lost brothers from the house of Israel. It forms an intrinsic part of the Messianic Hope of Israel, yet even so, most Jews are utterly unaware of the identity or the whereabouts of their Israelite brothers today. Some few, including a number of senior Rabbis are even now working for the ultimate reconciliation and restoration of the two houses of Israel. However, for the vast majority of the Jewish nation, the question does not even arise, as their main concern is a mixture of simply making a decent living for themselves and their families, and plain survival in this competitive and dangerous world of ours. They are not looking for their brother's return, and thus, the way the parable describes Judah's attitude fits today's situation pretty well.

What did the father mean by saying; "your brother was dead and is alive again?"

We know that in reality the prodigal son was not dead, as he had to be alive to survive the famine and arrive at his father's house. So, what did the father mean by saying to his older son; *"your brother was dead?"* As always, we find that the Bible interprets itself, and we find the answer in God's instruction to Moses regarding the way to treat a wayward and rebellious son:

> "*[18] If a man has a stubborn and rebellious son who will not obey the voice of his father or the voice of his mother, and who, when they have chastened him, will not heed them, [19] then his father and his mother shall take hold of him and bring him out to the elders of his city, to the gate of his city. [20] And they shall say to the elders of his city, 'This son of ours is stubborn and rebellious; he will not obey our voice; he is a glutton and a drunkard.' [21] Then all the men of his city shall stone him to death with stones; so you shall put away the*

> *evil from among you, and all Israel shall hear and fear.* ²² *If a man has committed a sin deserving of death, and he is put to death, and you hang him on a tree,* ²³ *his body shall not remain overnight on the tree, but you shall surely bury him that day, so that you do not defile the land which the LORD your God is giving you as an inheritance; for he who is hanged is accursed of God."*
> (Deuteronomy 21:18-23 NKJV)

The prodigal son rebelled against his father's house, as he took his inheritance and wasted it with *'riotous'* living, according to the KJV. The Hebrew word for *'riotous'* is *'zalal,'* which also means *'glutton,' 'drunkard,'* and *'waster.'* Gesenius' Hebrew-Chaldee Lexicon interprets it as follows: *"one who squanders his own body."* Even the letters of *'zalal'* give us a further fascinating insight in the deep meaning of this word. All the letters of the Hebrew alphabet have not only an individual meaning, but they also each have their own numerical value and these values in turn have meaning also. Thus, even the letters and the numbers convey a picture of what lies beneath the surface of the text. "*Zalal*" is spelled זָלַל "*zayin-lamed-lamed.*" The letter *'zayin'* is the *'sword'* or *'to cut off.'* Lamed is *'the shepherd's staff* and *'learning'* or *'teaching.'* The full meaning therefore is that this rebellious son has "**cut himself off from the Shepherds staff and all that he has been taught**." The rebellious son in this parable is of course none other than Ephraim who represents the Lost House of Israel. Moses speaks of the Ten Tribes of Israel in the same terms e.g. those of a rebellious son. This means that according to Torah Ephraim, has earned the penalty of the rebellious son. This punishment was to be "death" and the body was to be hung on a tree.

The good news is that, as in the example of the parable, God the Father never gave up on that son. Our Abba saw us while we were yet far off; while we were trying to find our way home, and He had compassion on us. He sent His own Son in the flesh to die the death of the rebellious son. He was hung on a tree and yet taken down before sundown and buried that same day, exactly as Torah prescribes. That is why the father in the parable was able to exclaim to his other son Judah:

> "[31] ...***Son, you are always with me, and all that I have is yours.*** [32] ***It was right that we should make merry and be glad, for your brother was dead and is alive again, and was lost and is found!***"
> (Luke: 15:31-32, NKJV)

We have seen how the real meaning of the parable was deliberately disguised and kept secret, as Yeshua only ever intended it for His true set apart disciples. Generally, most of us do not look for some subtext or hidden meaning, nevertheless; going by Yeshua's own words, there is a hidden meaning. We have also discovered that the key to understanding the hidden message in any parable lies in Yeshua's words to His disciples when He said to them:

> ***"To you it has been given to know the MYSTERY of the kingdom of God."***
> (Luke 8:10, emphasis added, NKJV)

We now understand that the mysteries of the Kingdom of God concern the revelation of the restoration of the two Houses of Israel into a United Kingdom. It is the time when the twelve tribes of Israel will once again be united into one Kingdom under the righteous rule of Messiah, the Son of David. The exciting news is that the Prodigal Son will return to his Father's House, and even today, we can discern the early green shoots of that great event becoming a marvellous reality.

HALLELUYAH!

Stephen J. Spykerman

The above was extracted from:
*"**CHRISTIANS & JEWS – THE TWO FACES OF ISRAEL**"*

To order your copy to get the rest of the story, visit: https://www.mountephraimwatchman.org/

BOOKS BY THE AUTHOR

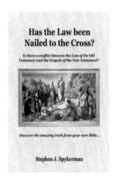

ABOUT THE AUTHOR

STEPHEN J. SPYKERMAN, was born the fourth son of a Dutch father and an English mother in September 1940 during the Nazi occupation of Holland. The family escaped the Holocaust due to his parent's Catholic religion plus the fact that his mother was English and thus, she was seen as English rather than the Jewish woman. Stephen's early years were full of excitement and danger, as their house for some time became the emergency headquarters for the Dutch resistance in his region. His father was arrested by the Nazi authorities and held for some time in a special prison for people who were considered influential in their local communities. His parents also sheltered Henny Cohen, a Jewish woman, who was hiding whilst on the run from the Nazi's. At the same time their formidable children's nanny worked as a courier for the Dutch resistance.

Having received a solid general education, Stephen spurned the higher education his parents had hoped for and entered the world of retail fashion at the age of nineteen. He eventually left his hometown to try his luck in London, where he followed a generations old family tradition by becoming a tailor in a variety of high-class fashion houses. In 1965, he married Virginia

Edwards. In time, he left the fashion industry and took up a more lucrative career in financial services. During his successful career, he pioneered a number of new schemes and concepts in charitable giving and seminar selling and became an international speaker in his field. His interest in public speaking led him to direct his own public speaking club. He, together with a colleague, he founded An International Speakers Bureau in London.

Stephen has a special love for and interest in the State of Israel. He is one of the earliest Members of the Temple Institute in Jerusalem. He was in at the inauguration of 'COI' - The Commonwealth Of Israel, by Moderating their first Conference in Jerusalem in May 2016, and subsequently became its Co-Founder. He then resigned from the organization in August 2017. COI's purpose was to foster reconciliation between Ephraim, the so called Lost Tribes of the House of Israel, and the House of Judah.

Once retired from day to day business, Stephen founded Mount Ephraim Publishing in 1998 and started writing books and to this day continues to give lectures on his research. Stephen Spykerman has addressed audiences and conferences all over Europe, Israel and North America. "**The Prodigal Son**" is his ninth book to date, published by Mount Ephraim Publishing in the United Kingdom in 2018, where it is available through Stephen's website:
https://www.mountephraimwatchman.org/

It may be obtained in the U.S. through Amazon.